PRESIDENTS

WILLIAM HOWARD TAFT

A MyReportLinks.com Book

Kim A. O'Connell

MyReportLinks.com Books
an imprint of
Enslow Publishers, Inc.
Box 398, 40 Industrial Road
Berkeley Heights, NJ 07922
USA

MyReportLinks.com Books, an imprint of Enslow Publishers, Inc. MyReportLinks is a trademark of Enslow Publishers, Inc.

Copyright © 2003 by Enslow Publishers, Inc.

All rights reserved.

No part of this book may be reproduced by any means without the written permission of the publisher.

Library of Congress Cataloging-in-Publication Data

O'Connell, Kim A.
  William Howard Taft / Kim A. O'Connell.
     p. cm. — (Presidents)
  Summary: Traces the life of the twenty-seventh president, who worked to guard against unfair child labor practices and oversaw the planting of the first Japanese cherry trees in Washington, D.C. Includes Internet links to Web sites, source documents, and photographs related to William Howard Taft.
  Includes bibliographical references and index.
  ISBN 0-7660-5078-5
  1. Taft, William H. (William Howard), 1857–1930—Juvenile literature.
  2. Presidents—United States—Biography—Juvenile literature. [1. Taft, William H. (William Howard), 1857–1930. 2. Presidents.] I. Title. II. Series.

  E762 .O28 2002
  973.91'2'092—dc21

2002000115

Printed in the United States of America

10 9 8 7 6 5 4 3 2 1

To Our Readers:
Through the purchase of this book, you and your library gain access to the Report Links that specifically back this book.
  The Publisher will provide access to the Report Links that back up this book and will keep these Report Links up to date on **www.myreportlinks.com** for three years from the book's first publication date.
  We have done our best to make sure all Internet addresses in this book were active and appropriate when we went to press. However, the author and the Publisher have no control over, and assume no liability for, the material available on those Internet sites or on other Web sites they may link to.
  The usage of the **MyReportLinks.com** Books Web site is subject to the terms and conditions stated on the Usage Policy Statement on www.myreportlinks.com.
  In the future, a password may be required to access the Report Links that back up this book. The password can be found on the bottom of page 4 of this book.
  Any comments or suggestions can be sent by e-mail to comments@myreportlinks.com or to the address on the back cover.

Photo Credits: © Corel Corporation, pp. 1 (background), 3; American Memory, The Library of Congress, pp. 28, 32; MyReportLinks.com Books, p. 4; The Library of Congress, pp. 1, 11, 12, 34, 40; The National Park Service, William Howard Taft Historic Site, pp. 14, 16, 17, 18, 37; The Ohio State University, p. 24; The Smithsonian Institution, pp. 30, 42; The Supreme Court of the United States, p. 38; The United States Department of the Interior, pp. 26, 35; The White House Historical Association, p. 22.

Cover Photo: © Corel Corporation; The Library of Congress.

Contents

Report Links 4

Highlights 10

1 The Reluctant President 11

2 Learning the Law: Taft's Early Life,
   1857–1880 14

3 The Way to the White House,
   1880–1908 21

4 A Stiff Upper Lip: The Presidency,
   1909–1913 28

5 From Yale to the Supreme Court,
   1913–1930 36

6 Last Years and Legacy 41

   Chapter Notes 45

   Further Reading 47

   Index 48

About MyReportLinks.com Books

MyReportLinks.com Books
Great Books, Great Links, Great for Research!

MyReportLinks.com Books present the information you need to learn about your report subject. In addition, they show you where to go on the Internet for more information. The pre-evaluated Report Links that back up this book are kept up to date on **www.myreportlinks.com**. With the purchase of a MyReportLinks.com Books title, you and your library gain access to the Report Links that specifically back up that book. The Report Links save hours of research time and link to dozens—even hundreds—of Web sites, source documents, and photos related to your report topic.

Please see "To Our Readers" on the Copyright page for important information about this book, the MyReportLinks.com Books Web site, and the Report Links that back up this book.

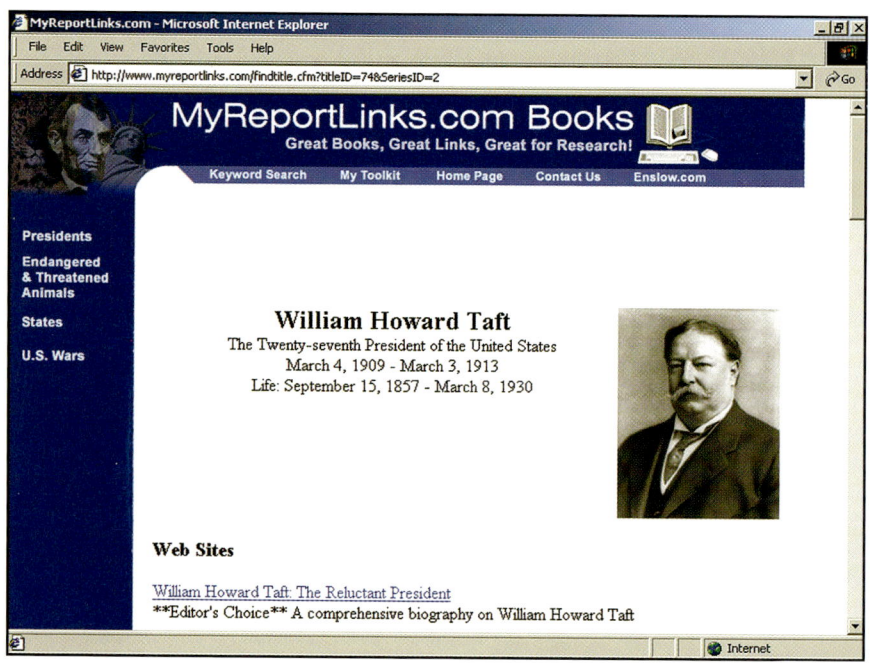

Access:

The Publisher will provide access to the Report Links that back up this book and will try to keep these Report Links up to date on our Web site for three years from the book's first publication date. Please enter **PTA5279** if asked for a password.

MyReportLinks.com Books

Tools Search Notes Discuss Go!

Report Links

▶ The Internet sites described below can be accessed at http://www.myreportlinks.com

*Editor's choice

▶ **William Howard Taft: The Reluctant President**
This comprehensive Web site provides detailed information about President William Howard Taft. Here you will learn about his early life, presidential campaigns, domestic and foreign affairs, the First Lady, and his legacy. You will also find images, quotes, and additional resources.
Link to this Internet site from http://www.myreportlinks.com

*Editor's choice

▶ **William Howard Taft**
This Web site provides facts and figures on William Howard Taft. Here you will find election results, cabinet appointments, information about Taft's family and important events in his administration, and other Internet resources.
Link to this Internet site from http://www.myreportlinks.com

*Editor's choice

▶ **The American Presidency: William Howard Taft**
This Web site offers a biography of William Howard Taft. Here you will learn about his early life, governorship of the Philippines, career as secretary of war, the presidency, and his final years as chief justice of the United States.
Link to this Internet site from http://www.myreportlinks.com

*Editor's choice

▶ **"I Do Solemnly Swear . . ."**
By navigating through this site you can experience the inauguration of William Howard Taft. Here you will find photographs documenting the day, his inaugural address, and memorabilia.

Link to this Internet site from http://www.myreportlinks.com

*Editor's choice

▶ **Cherry Trees Planted in Washington, D.C.**
America's Story from America's Library, a Library of Congress Web site, tells the story of Helen Herron Taft's role in the planting of the cherry trees that line the Tidal Basin in Washington, D.C.

Link to this Internet site from http://www.myreportlinks.com

*Editor's choice

▶ **American Presidents: Life Portraits—William Howard Taft**
At this Web site you will find "Life Facts" and trivia about William Howard Taft. You will also find a letter written by Taft to Judge William Worthington regarding Taft's situation in the Philippines.

Link to this Internet site from http://www.myreportlinks.com

Any comments? Contact us: comments@myreportlinks.com

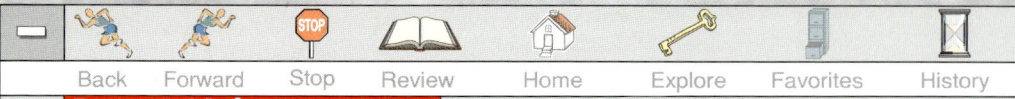

Report Links

The Internet sites described below can be accessed at
http://www.myreportlinks.com

▶ The American Presidency: Helen Herron Taft
At this Web site you will find a brief profile of Helen Herron Taft, including some of her experiences as First Lady and her personal interests.

Link to this Internet site from http://www.myreportlinks.com

▶ Growing Into Public Service: William Howard Taft's Boyhood Home
Here you will find images, articles, and documents related to William Howard Taft's boyhood and family. In addition to reading about Taft's birthplace, you can take the test that Taft took to gain admittance to high school.

Link to this Internet site from http://www.myreportlinks.com

▶ The Supreme Court
The official Web site of the Supreme Court of the United States includes archival photographs of the Court's home over the years. Here you can see a photo of the Old Senate Chamber in the Capitol, which is where the Court met when Taft presided as chief justice from 1921 to 1930.

Link to this Internet site from http://www.myreportlinks.com

▶ James S. Sherman
This Web site provides a brief overview of William Howard Taft's vice president, James Schoolcraft Sherman.

Link to this Internet site from http://www.myreportlinks.com

▶ Mr. President: William Howard Taft
At this Web site you will find a brief profile of William Howard Taft and an interesting quotation from Taft about politics.

Link to this Internet site from http://www.myreportlinks.com

▶ Objects from the Presidency
By navigating through this site you will find objects related to all the United States presidents, including William Howard Taft. You can also read a brief description of the era he lived in and learn about the office of the presidency.

Link to this Internet site from http://www.myreportlinks.com

Any comments? Contact us: comments@myreportlinks.com

▶ **The Panama Canal: A Brief History**
At this Web site you will find a brief history of the Panama Canal and William Howard Taft's role in its development.

▶ **Potomac Blossoms**
At this Library of Congress Web site you will learn about the cherry trees that were planted along the Potomac River Tidal Basin in Washington, D.C., by Helen Herron Taft.

▶ **Resource Extraction on the Delta**
This article explains in detail the environmental policies of Roosevelt and Taft and the reasons for a rift in their friendship.

▶ **The Taft Family in Japan**
At the Connect Ohio Web site you will find information regarding the Taft family's continuing relationship with Japan, which began in 1900 with William Howard Taft.

▶ **Taft Gained Peaks In Unusual Career**
At this Web site you will find the *New York Times* obituary of William Howard Taft.

▶ **Taft, Robert Alphonso (1889–1953)**
At the Biographical Directory of the United States Congress Web site, you will find a biography of Robert Alphonso Taft, son of President William Howard Taft, who served as a United States senator from 1939 to 1953.

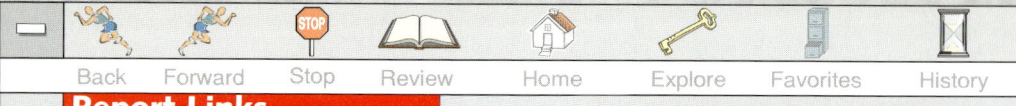

Report Links

The Internet sites described below can be accessed at
http://www.myreportlinks.com

▶**Taft, William Howard**
At this Web site you will find a biography of William Howard Taft. In addition you will also find election results and the text of four of his speeches.

Link to this Internet site from http://www.myreportlinks.com

▶**Theodore Roosevelt (1858–1919)
Receives Majority of Washington Votes . . .**
Here you will find an article about the presidential election of 1912, one of the most unusual in the history of the United States.

Link to this Internet site from http://www.myreportlinks.com

▶**U.S. Presidents 1889–1953**
By navigating through this Web site you will find the biographies of William Howard Taft and other presidents. You will also find quotations and a listing of historic presidential places.

Link to this Internet site from http://www.myreportlinks.com

▶**The White House: Helen Herron Taft**
The official White House Web site holds the biography of First Lady Helen Herron Taft. Here you will learn about her courtship with Taft, her life in the White House, and other information about the Taft family.

Link to this Internet site from http://www.myreportlinks.com

▶**The White House Historical Association**
At the White House Historical Association you can explore the rich history of the White House and the presidents of the United States. You can also take a virtual tour of the White House, visit President's Park, and experience past presidential inaugurations.

Link to this Internet site from http://www.myreportlinks.com

▶**The White House: William Howard Taft**
The official White House Web site holds the biography of William Howard Taft. Here you will learn how Taft was viewed as a politician and how he felt about being president.

Link to this Internet site from http://www.myreportlinks.com

Any comments? Contact us: comments@myreportlinks.com

Tools Search Notes Discuss   Go!

Report Links

 The Internet sites described below can be accessed at
http://www.myreportlinks.com

▶ **William Howard Taft**
This Web site provides a brief biography of William Howard Taft. You will also find interesting facts, quotations, and information about his administration and cabinet members.

Link to this Internet site from http://www.myreportlinks.com

▶ **William Howard Taft (1857–1930)**
At the National Portrait Gallery Web site you can view a painting of William Howard Taft and read a brief profile of Taft.

Link to this Internet site from http://www.myreportlinks.com

▶ **William Howard Taft: Defense of a Higher Tariff**
At this Web site you will find William Howard Taft's speech defending his support for the Payne-Aldrich Tariff Act. This bill divided the Republican Party and caused conflict between Taft and Theodore Roosevelt.

Link to this Internet site from http://www.myreportlinks.com

▶ **William Howard Taft: Inaugural Address**
At this Web site you will find the complete text of President William Howard Taft's inaugural address, which he delivered on Thursday, March 4, 1909.

Link to this Internet site from http://www.myreportlinks.com

▶ **William Howard Taft National Historic Site**
At this Web site you will find a brief description and photograph of Taft's childhood home, now the William Howard Taft National Historic Site, in Mount Auburn, Ohio (a suburb of Cincinnati).

Link to this Internet site from http://www.myreportlinks.com

▶ **1912: Competing Visions for America**
This Web site explores the presidential election of 1912. Here you will learn about the candidates, the issues, and the outcome.

Link to this Internet site from http://www.myreportlinks.com

Any comments? Contact us: comments@myreportlinks.com

Highlights

1857—*Sept. 15:* Born in Cincinnati, Ohio.

1874—Graduates second in his high school class.

1878—Earns B.A. from Yale University, again placing second in his class.

1880—Graduates from University of Cincinnati Law School.

1881—Appointed assistant prosecutor for Hamilton County, Ohio.

1882—Appointed collector of internal revenue for Ohio's First District.

1886—*June 19:* Marries Helen "Nellie" Herron.

1887—Appointed to Superior Court of Ohio.

1889—First son, Robert, is born.

1890—Appointed U.S. Solicitor General.

1891—First daughter, Helen, is born.

1892—Appointed judge of the Sixth U.S. Circuit Court.

1897—Second son and last child, Charles, is born.

1900—Appointed president of the Philippines governing commission.

1901—Appointed governor-general of the Philippines by President McKinley.

1904—Appointed secretary of war by President Theodore Roosevelt.

1908—*Nov. 3:* Elected twenty-seventh president of the United States.

1909—*Aug. 5:* Signs Payne-Aldrich Tariff bill.

1912—Loses reelection bid to Woodrow Wilson.

—Approves addition of New Mexico and Arizona as states.

1913—Becomes law professor at Yale University.

1921—Appointed chief justice of the United States.

1930—*Feb. 3:* Retires as chief justice due to failing health.

1930—*March 8:* Dies in Washington, D.C.

Chapter 1

The Reluctant President

In early 1908, William Howard Taft was finally back in the United States after a long trip the previous fall. He and his wife, Nellie, and their ten-year-old son Charlie, had traveled around the world, visiting Japan, the Philippines, and Russia. Now that the family had returned, Taft wondered what the next step in his career would be. After a lifetime of public service, William Howard Taft was not sure whether to run for political office or to seek an appointment to the United States Supreme Court, his lifelong goal.

The Tafts wanted to talk about the dilemma over dinner at the home of their good friends Theodore and Edith Roosevelt. But the Roosevelts' home was not like any other home—it was the White House. Roosevelt was president of the United States.

Roosevelt did not want to run for president again, and it was no secret that he wanted Taft to follow in his footsteps. On that cold January night, the

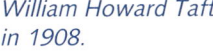

William Howard Taft in 1908.

cheerful Roosevelt decided to entertain his guests. He closed his eyes and began to chant as if he were a fortune-teller. "I see a man before me weighing about 350 pounds," Roosevelt said, teasing Taft about his large size. "There is something hanging over his head. I cannot make out what it is; it is hanging by a slender thread. At one time it looks like the Presidency—then again it looks like the Chief Justiceship."[1]

Before Roosevelt could continue, Taft's wife, Nellie, made her choice known. "Make it the presidency!" Nellie said. But Taft had always seen himself in the

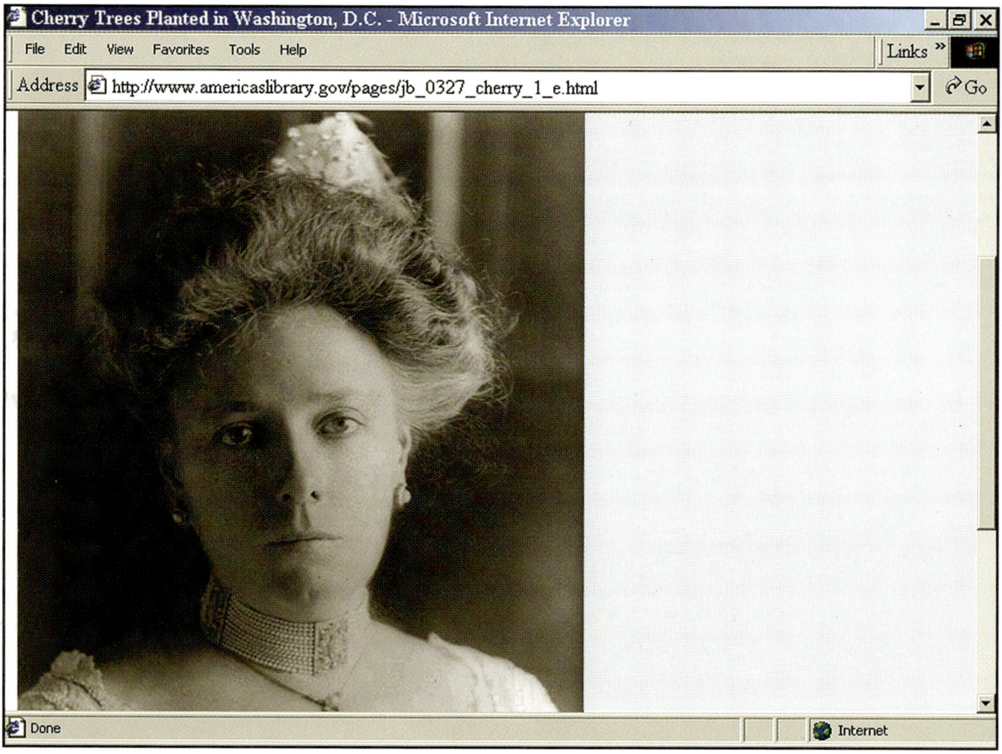

▲ Helen Herron Taft, known as Nellie. Taft was persuaded to run for the presidency by his wife, whom he referred to as "the politician" in the family.

robes of the Supreme Court. He replied, "Make it the Chief Justiceship!"[2]

In the end, Nellie's choice won. Taft began campaigning for president, although he was not as comfortable in the spotlight as Roosevelt had been. Taft was warm and friendly, but a very private man. He quickly tired of all the publicity and the cameras snapping in his face. Taft was sometimes so worn out after campaigning that he fell asleep in cars, restaurants, and other public places.

To make matters worse, Taft was criticized for letting Roosevelt take over his campaign. Taft was happy to receive guidance from his friend, but Taft's wife and others felt that Roosevelt was too involved. A common joke heard during that time was that "TAFT" stood for "Take Advice from Theodore."[3] Eventually, Roosevelt and Taft would grow to resent each other—leading to the breakup of one of the most famous friendships in American history.

That November, Taft won the White House. Even as he prepared to be the nation's twenty-seventh president, he felt nervous about his new role. Yet he knew that his wife Nellie would be ready to offer advice. "If I were now presiding in the Supreme Court of the United States as chief justice, I should feel entirely at home," Taft wrote to a friend. But as president, Taft said, "I feel just a bit like a fish out of water. However, as my wife is the politician and she will be able to meet all these issues, perhaps we can keep a stiff upper lip."[4]

Taft had achieved the highest public office in the land, but his dream was still out of reach.

Chapter 2 ▶

Learning the Law: Taft's Early Life, 1857–1880

In 1857 the streets and shops of Cincinnati, Ohio, were bustling. Boats on the Ohio River and railroads moved cargo in and out of the growing city. Playhouses showing comedies and magic shows were packed with people. In the surrounding hills, spacious homes reflected the city's rising status. One of these homes belonged to Alphonso and Louise Taft.

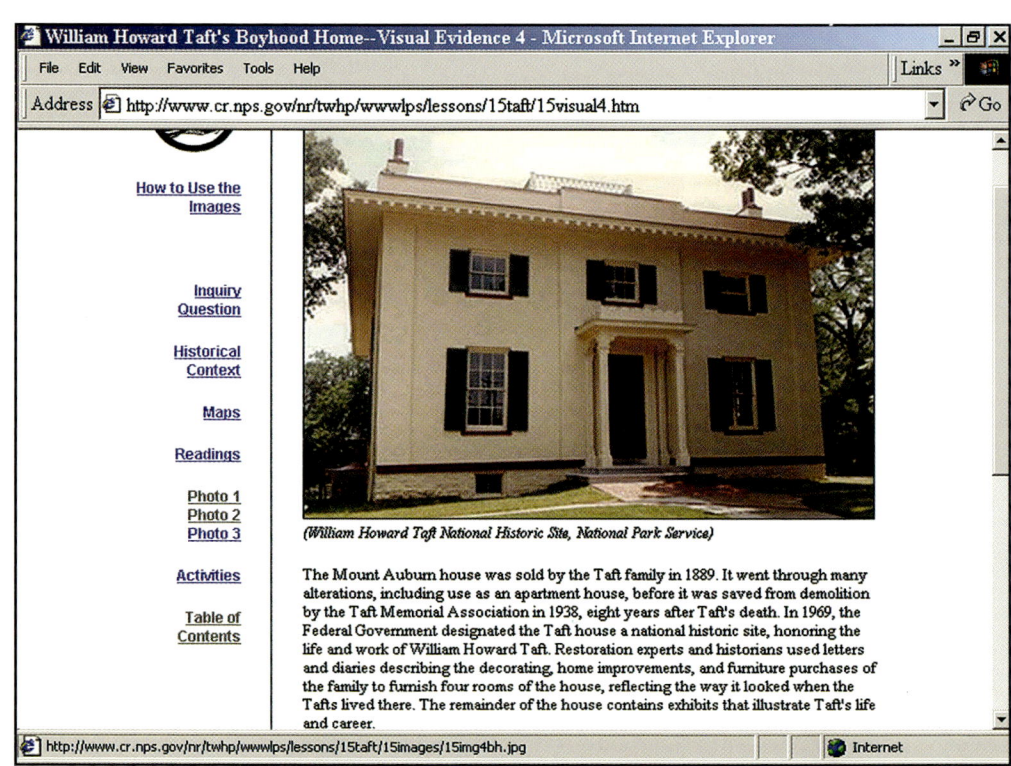

▲ The Taft homestead, in the Mount Auburn section of Cincinnati, Ohio, where William Howard Taft grew up. It was designated a national historic site in 1969.

Alphonso Taft had worked his way up from a frugal childhood in Vermont to become a prominent lawyer and judge in Cincinnati. The Tafts were well-liked and respected, and they held many parties. Although they were not as rich as some of their friends, their home was furnished with a marble-top table and a piano in the parlor. Louise was anxious to please her husband, whose first wife had died five years before. On one New Year's Eve, Louise impressed her guests by wearing a green-and-black silk gown. In public, she always called her husband "Mr. Taft."

On September 15, 1857, William Howard Taft was born to Alphonso and Louise Taft. He was the first of their sons to survive past infancy, joining two sons from Alphonso's previous marriage. Because their first child had died of whooping cough at only a year old, Louise was happy to see that young Willie, as she called him, was healthy and growing fatter every day. At only seven weeks old, Willie had already outgrown the baby clothes Louise's mother had sewn for him. "He has such a large waist that he cannot wear any of the dresses that are made with belts," Louise wrote to her sister. But she clearly loved her new son very much, adding, "Our little Willie is well and hearty and a most charming baby as you would wish to see."[1]

▶ A Top Student

When Will entered public school in Cincinnati in 1863, he had grown tall and stout. He had also grown tough. Neighborhood boys called him "Lub" or "Lubber" to tease him about his weight, which made Will work even harder to succeed at school and on the playing field. He often led stone-throwing battles against bullies in the neighborhood.

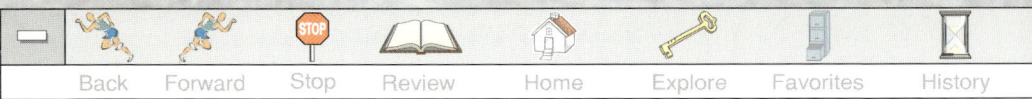

▲ This photograph captures young William Howard Taft (holding the pony's reins) with his two half brothers and their pony in front of the family's barn. Taft also had two brothers and a sister from his father's second marriage.

Baseball became a favorite sport, too, and Will covered second base with a quick, strong arm.

But what made Will Taft work hard at everything he tried was his desire to please his parents, especially his father. Will rarely felt that even his best efforts were good enough for Alphonso. And indeed, his father once said, "Mediocrity will not do for Will."[2] Eager to please his parents, the young Taft was first in his class by December 1869.

By the time he finished his senior year of high school

Learning the Law: Taft's Early Life

in June 1874, Will was second in his class, which made him salutatorian. Already aware of politics, Will gave his graduation speech about women's suffrage, the movement to allow women the right to vote.

▶ College Years

That September, Will chose the college that his father and two older half brothers had attended, Yale University, in New Haven, Connecticut. His talent at sports and studies stayed with him at Yale, although he complained about the hard benches in the school chapel and the boring sermons. Although he was well-liked, Will was sometimes so serious

▲ *William Howard Taft is seen here (first row, center, wearing hat) with his graduating class from Woodward High School.*

Alphonso Taft was a great influence in his son's life. The elder Taft served as both secretary of war and attorney general in the Grant administration.

about his pursuits that he lost his temper. One night during his senior year, two rowdy friends would not leave him alone to study, so Taft angrily threw books, pillows, and other items at them until they left.

Will's name became even better known in 1876, when his father was named secretary of war and attorney general under President Ulysses S. Grant. Will soon became more interested in politics himself. Like his half brother Peter, Will was invited, while he was a junior, to join Yale's Skull and Bones Society when he became a senior. This secret society on the Yale campus was made up of politically minded young men from prominent families. Will's father had helped to found the society.

In 1878, Taft graduated from Yale, again second in his class, again the salutatorian. His political thoughts were sharper than ever. His speech was titled "The Professional and Political Prospects of the College Graduate." Will already had ideas about his own professional and political prospects.

Turning to the Law

After graduation, Taft spent the summer reading law in his father's office before entering the University of Cincinnati Law School in the fall. Although he worked hard at his job, he still loved sports. One day, he decided to watch a Yale boat race rather than stay home and study. When Alphonso found out, he scolded his son in a letter. "I do not think you have accomplished as much this past year as you ought with your opportunities," the elder Taft wrote. "I like to have you enjoy yourself, so far as it can be consistent with your success in life."[3]

To gain experience, Taft took a job as a part-time court reporter for a local newspaper, the *Cincinnati Commercial*. He covered all the county and federal courts during the day and wrote as many as five or six articles before going home at night. Taft's editor liked his work so much that he offered him a good salary if he would give up law for journalism. But Taft knew he wanted to practice law and turned down the offer. In 1880, Taft graduated from law school and was admitted to the Ohio bar. He was soon appointed assistant prosecutor for Hamilton County, Ohio. His first case involved a maid who had stolen $35 from her employer. From there, Taft went on to prosecute more serious cases, including murder cases.

▶ The Lure of Politics

Although Taft was finally doing what he loved to do, he could not ignore national politics. His father was a respected member of the Republican Party, and Taft was expected to do his part for the party as well. In the summer and fall of 1880, Taft traveled around the state, campaigning for various Republican political candidates. He did not yet foresee that he would one day be a candidate himself.

Chapter 3 ▶ The Way to the White House, 1880–1908

In January 1882, Judge Alphonso Taft got a sense of how powerful his son was becoming. President Chester A. Arthur had just appointed the judge ambassador to Austria-Hungary. But to the surprise of the Taft family, President Arthur also appointed the younger Taft collector of internal revenue for the first district of Ohio. Almost immediately, Taft was introduced to favoritism and corruption in politics. A congressman asked Taft to fire several men in the internal revenue department so that friends of the Republican Party could be hired instead. But Taft defended the men and refused to fire them, showing the honesty and integrity that came to mark his career. "I do not want to have any hand in it," Taft said. "I would much rather resign and let someone else do [the congressman's] dirty work."[1] That December, Taft did resign, joining a law firm headed by a former associate of his father.

But it was not all work. The following summer, Taft took a tour of Europe, visiting his parents in Vienna, Austria, where his father was serving as ambassador. He also hiked through Switzerland with a childhood friend and visited Ireland, Scotland, and England. But Taft was eager to return home for two reasons. For one, he was rapidly running out of money. But he also was unable to stop thinking about a girl named Helen Herron, also known as Nellie, whom he had met at a party back in 1879.

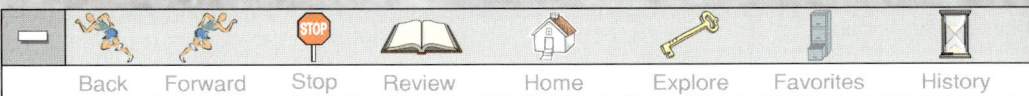

A Suitable Match

The daughter of a Cincinnati lawyer, Nellie was raised in an atmosphere of intelligence and social grace. Nellie loved to read and invited Taft to join a book club that she hosted. At first, they were just friends who both loved books. Taft soon found that he loved Nellie, too.

But before Taft could propose to Nellie, he was faced with the first major legal battle of his life. A corrupt lawyer, Thomas Campbell, was being tried in Cincinnati for using threats and other illegal means to free his clients from the

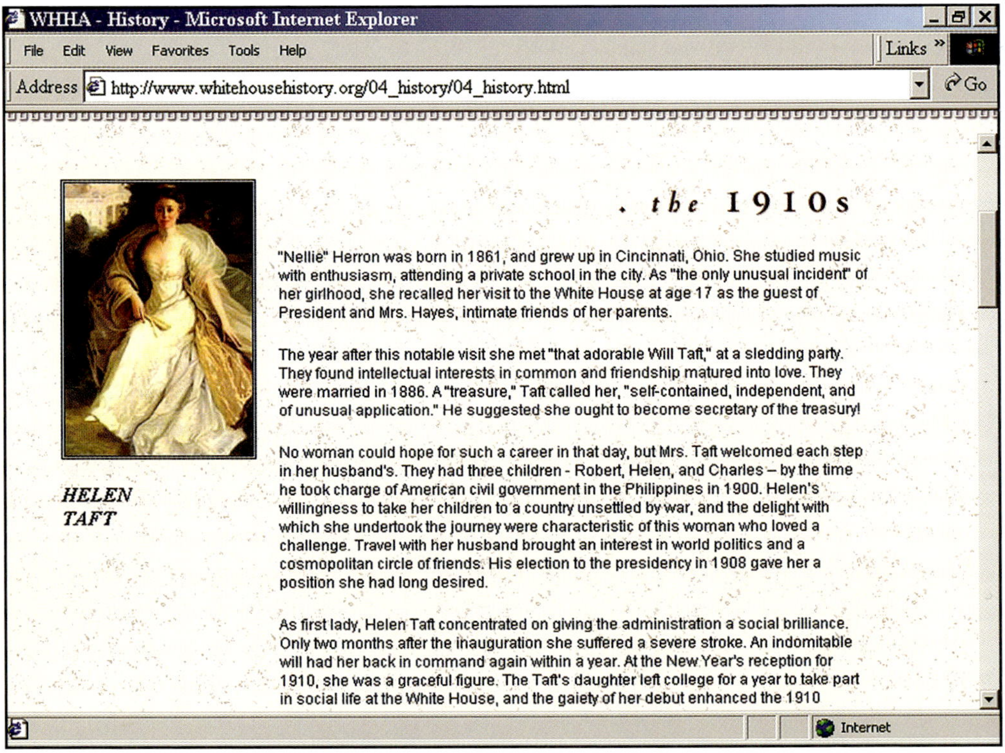
WHHA - History - Microsoft Internet Explorer

File Edit View Favorites Tools Help Links

Address http://www.whitehousehistory.org/04_history/04_history.html Go

HELEN TAFT

. the 1910s

"Nellie" Herron was born in 1861, and grew up in Cincinnati, Ohio. She studied music with enthusiasm, attending a private school in the city. As "the only unusual incident" of her girlhood, she recalled her visit to the White House at age 17 as the guest of President and Mrs. Hayes, intimate friends of her parents.

The year after this notable visit she met "that adorable Will Taft," at a sledding party. They found intellectual interests in common and friendship matured into love. They were married in 1886. A "treasure," Taft called her, "self-contained, independent, and of unusual application." He suggested she ought to become secretary of the treasury!

No woman could hope for such a career in that day, but Mrs. Taft welcomed each step in her husband's. They had three children - Robert, Helen, and Charles – by the time he took charge of American civil government in the Philippines in 1900. Helen's willingness to take her children to a country unsettled by war, and the delight with which she undertook the journey were characteristic of this woman who loved a challenge. Travel with her husband brought an interest in world politics and a cosmopolitan circle of friends. His election to the presidency in 1908 gave her a position she had long desired.

As first lady, Helen Taft concentrated on giving the administration a social brilliance. Only two months after the inauguration she suffered a severe stroke. An indomitable will had her back in command again within a year. At the New Year's reception for 1910, she was a graceful figure. The Taft's daughter left college for a year to take part in social life at the White House, and the gaiety of her debut enhanced the 1910

Internet

Helen Herron, the daughter of a Cincinnati lawyer, met William Howard Taft at a sledding party in 1879. The two became friends and finally married in 1886. The Tafts had three children: Robert, Helen, and Charles.

court system. Public outrage over Campbell's misdeeds led to riots in the streets. In March 1884, a mob burned the courthouse, destroying Taft's beloved law library. Taft was hired to prosecute Campbell. Although Taft's speeches in the courtroom impressed many people, he still lost the case. Taft was so upset by this loss that he threatened to give up his career, but his father encouraged him to continue practicing law.

After more than a year of courting, Nellie Herron finally agreed to marry William Howard Taft. She even wrote him a little valentine:

> St. Valentine the good!
> Now cheer & cheer him still
> For giving Will to Nellie
> And giving Nellie to Will.[2]

On June 19, 1886, Taft married Nellie at the Herron home. After a honeymoon in France, England, and Scotland, the couple settled in their new house in Cincinnati. They entertained often, and friends began to notice that Nellie could be critical of her new husband. She disapproved of him often, even as she urged him toward higher and higher political office. And Taft began to rely on her for guidance just as he had with his parents when he was a child. "I know that I am very cross to you," Nellie once wrote him, "but I love you just the same."[3]

▶ The New Judge

The following year, Taft was appointed to fill a seat on the Ohio Superior Court. He performed his duties so well that the governor of Ohio and other Republicans urged President Benjamin Harrison to appoint Taft to the United States Supreme Court. But the appointment was unlikely because Taft was still young. "My chances of going to the moon and of donning a silk gown," Taft wrote, referring to the robes of the high court, ". . . are about equal."[4]

Instead, Taft was offered the position of United States Solicitor General. In this position, Taft would be required to argue cases in an open courtroom, just as he had with the Campbell case. But after that loss, he was not confident about his abilities. Taft wanted to decline the offer, which would mean a move to Washington, D.C., but Nellie convinced him to accept it. Once in the nation's

▲ William Howard Taft became the Republican Party's presidential nominee in 1908. This photograph shows Taft accepting the nomination. As was the custom of the day, the nominee did not attend his party's convention but was notified by a committee that he had won.

capital, Taft made the best of it. He quickly became friends with Theodore Roosevelt, who was then the civil service commissioner. The two men lived close to each other, and they often walked to work together and met for lunch. The Tafts set up a small home in the heart of the city, furnishing it with ample shelves for all their books. In September 1889, the Tafts' first child, Robert, was born. The following August, their daughter, Helen, was born.

As he had expected, Taft did not enjoy being solicitor general and successfully campaigned for a seat on the Sixth U.S. Circuit Court of Appeals, which brought him back to his beloved Cincinnati. Taft gave his all to his new position, going over cases in painstaking detail. His fairness earned him praise from the Republican Party. Nellie found Cincinnati society less active than that of Washington, D.C. Still, she kept herself busy with classes and volunteer work, and she gave birth to their third child, Charles, in 1897.

To the Philippines and Beyond

The following year, the United States plunged into the Spanish-American War, which was fought over Spain's interests in Cuba. The war ended in December 1898 with the signing of a treaty with Spain. The treaty resulted in the United States gaining control of lands that Spain once held, including Cuba, Puerto Rico, Guam, and the Philippines, a chain of Asian islands. On a January afternoon in 1900, Taft received an unexpected telegram from President William McKinley, asking him to lead a governing commission for the Philippines. Taft hesitated until McKinley promised him that he would one day serve on the Supreme Court. Taft left for the islands, where the people quickly impressed him. The following year, he became civil governor of the Philippines, helping to establish local governments and repair roads and other facilities. And because he thought it was his responsibility to guide the Philippines through an economic crisis, Taft even turned down two later offers, in 1902 and 1903, to be appointed to the Supreme Court.

But history was about to take a dramatic turn. In September 1901, President McKinley was assassinated, and Theodore Roosevelt, the vice president and Taft's friend, succeeded McKinley as president. Taft had already been sick when he was further upset by the news of McKinley's death. At more than 320 pounds, Taft was the heaviest he had ever been, and the heat of the Philippines was too much for him. With his family, he sailed home to recuperate, just in time for Christmas.

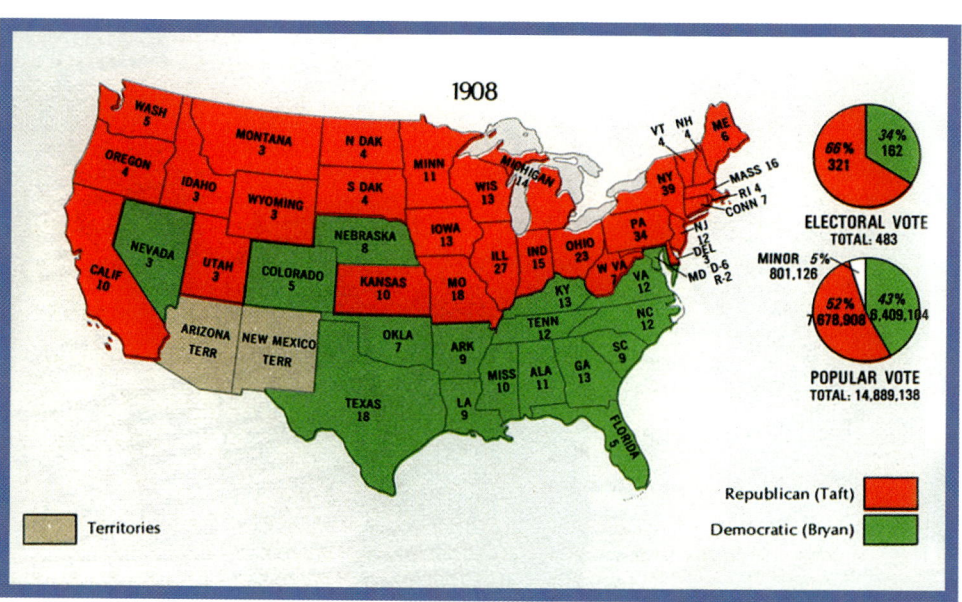

▲ This map shows the presidential election results of 1908. The states in red were won by Taft, who managed to capture 66% of the electoral vote and 52% of the popular vote in defeating his opponent, William Jennings Bryan.

▶ Groomed for the Presidency

By 1904, Taft was ready for a new challenge. He accepted an offer from President Roosevelt to serve in his cabinet as secretary of war. As such, Taft was put in charge of the construction of the Panama Canal. Roosevelt piled on additional duties, grooming Taft for the presidency. Between 1905 and 1906, Taft even went on a strict diet, dropping from 320 to 250 pounds.

It was no surprise to political observers that in 1908, Taft was nominated for the presidency on the Republican ticket. Throughout Taft's campaign, however, Roosevelt remained a very popular figure. In fact, the applause at the Republican National Convention lasted longer for Roosevelt than for Taft—which annoyed Nellie Taft greatly. But riding the wave of Roosevelt's popularity, Taft was elected president by an electoral vote of 321 to 162.

Chapter 4 ▶

A Stiff Upper Lip: The Presidency, 1909–1913

Inauguration Day—March 4, 1909—dawned blustery, icy, and cold. The conditions were so miserable that Taft's inauguration ceremony was forced indoors to the Senate chamber. The weather was an accurate reflection of the stormy political times to follow. Already, the first crack

▲ Taft and outgoing president Theodore Roosevelt are seen in this photograph driving through the snow-covered streets of Washington, D.C., to the Capitol for Taft's inauguration. Because of the weather—ten inches of snow fell that day—Taft's inaugural ceremony took place inside the Capitol.

in the Taft-Roosevelt friendship appeared when Taft decided to choose his own cabinet members, instead of keeping Roosevelt's choices. But the night before the inaugural, the two friends spent the evening together at the White House.

Taft devoted his inaugural address to the issues he cared about, including building up the United States armed forces, fostering prosperity in the Philippines, and securing the right of blacks in the South to vote. He made a verbal bow to Roosevelt as well. It was his honor, Taft said, to have served under Theodore Roosevelt and helped to advance his reforms, especially regarding abuses of power in the railroads and other large corporations. "I should be untrue to myself, to my promises, and to the declarations of the party platform on which I was elected to office," Taft said, "if I did not make the maintenance and enforcement of those reforms a most important feature of my administration."[1]

Soon after becoming president, Taft had the White House stables converted into a four-car garage. The large president also brought in a special bathtub big enough to hold four men. But even after he had made the White House his own, Taft was still being compared unfavorably with Roosevelt. This poem, which appeared in *Life* magazine, summed up the views of many that Taft lacked Roosevelt's appeal.

> Teddy, come home and blow your horn,
> The sheep's in the meadow, the cow's in the corn.
> The boy you left to tend the sheep
> Is under the haystack fast asleep.[2]

Things were about to get worse.

▶ Tough Times

Only two months after the inaugural, while on a yachting trip down the Potomac River, Nellie Taft suddenly fainted. She suffered a stroke, which left her unable to speak and barely able to move. Although Nellie eventually recovered after about a year, she was unable to support her husband in the critical first days of his presidency, when Taft needed guidance the most.

The first great challenge of Taft's presidency involved tariffs, which are taxes on imported goods. In 1909,

▲ Teddy Roosevelt had been known as the "Great Trust-Buster," but Taft was as diligent as his predecessor in enforcing antitrust laws. Both the American Tobacco Company and the Standard Oil trust were dismantled in 1911, during Taft's administration.

tariff rates were at the highest they had ever been. Taft had campaigned on the promise that he would make changes in the tariff rates. Some Republicans felt that those changes meant Taft would only restructure the tariff rate system. But others in the party felt that the change would be a tariff reduction. After intense debate in both the House of Representatives and the Senate, Taft signed a bill creating the Payne-Aldrich Tariff Act, which lowered some tariffs, raised others, and left some tariffs unchanged. It was a compromise, and Taft was criticized for not lowering tariffs enough. He drew further criticism when he called the act "the best tariff bill that the Republican Party has ever passed."[3]

The following year, the crack in the Taft-Roosevelt friendship widened further. Taft fired Gifford Pinchot, chief of the U.S. Forest Service, who had been one of Roosevelt's right-hand men. Pinchot had publicly attacked Richard Ballinger, whom Taft had appointed Secretary of the Department of the Interior. In addition to angering Roosevelt, Taft's firing of Pinchot brought about claims that Taft did not care about land conservation as much as Roosevelt did. Later, their friendship was all but doomed when Taft defended an antitrust lawsuit against U.S. Steel, a corporation that Roosevelt had supported. Although Roosevelt had been known as the "Great Trust-Buster," more trusts were prosecuted under Taft's administration than under Roosevelt's.

▶ Brighter Days

But the Tafts enjoyed plenty of happy moments in the White House. In June 1911, the Tafts celebrated their silver wedding anniversary. Nellie wanted a party in keeping with twenty-five years of marriage, and she got it. The

▲ Nellie Taft was instrumental in getting Japan to donate cherry trees to the nation's capital. Those trees were then planted along the Potomac Tidal Basin, and their spring blossoms are still an eagerly awaited annual event in Washington, D.C.

White House was lined with thousands of sparkling lights. Paper lanterns hung in the trees, and a spotlight shone on a large American flag. More than 3,400 guests attended, bringing many gifts. The Tafts received so many presents that, for many years afterward, Nellie would wrap up anniversary gifts to give to others as if they were brand-new. One gift that Mrs. Taft gave to the entire country, however, has endured to this day: She arranged for and oversaw the planting of the many Japanese cherry trees that line the Potomac River Tidal Basin, in the nation's capital.

In spring, when the trees are in full bloom, the cherry blossoms are a major tourist attraction.

▶ Presidential Successes

As president, Taft enjoyed several successes as well. In 1910, he signed into law the Mann-Elkins Act, which strengthened the Interstate Commerce Commission. The commission could now fix the maximum rates charged by railroads and was put in charge of the telephone and telegraph industries. In 1912, Taft urged the adoption of an annual federal budget. He created a secure postal savings-bank system, which protected investors from losing their money in unstable banks. He worked to guard children against unfair child-labor practices, and he established workers' compensation for railroad employees. Taft also appointed six justices to the United States Supreme Court, the most appointments by any president serving a single term.

Furthermore, Taft helped to expand the United States domestically and internationally. He oversaw the admission of New Mexico and Arizona as the forty-seventh and forty-eighth states, respectively. He pushed for free trade between Canada and the United States, and he signed a bill that freed American shipping fleets from paying Panama Canal tolls.

▶ The Bull Moose Strikes

As Taft faced reelection in 1912, however, the political winds were about to shift against him once and for all. Teddy Roosevelt, the man who had helped elect Taft in 1908, decided to run for president again. The views of Taft's former friend had become more liberal and in some cases radical since he left office. For example, Roosevelt felt that it was the right of citizens to overturn judges' decisions, an idea that Taft's judicial mind could not accept. Taft was not keen on another presidential term, but he did not want the radical Roosevelt in the White House either.

Roosevelt had stunned many of his former peers by breaking with the Republican Party and accepting the presidential nomination offered by the newly formed Progressive, or Bull Moose, Party. The Republicans nominated Taft again, but the Roosevelt candidacy split the Republican vote. As a result, the Democratic Party staged an easy win. That November, their candidate, Woodrow Wilson, was elected president, with Roosevelt earning the second highest number of votes. Taft came in third.

Former president—and former friend to William Howard Taft—Theodore Roosevelt chose to run for a third term as a third-party candidate in the 1912 presidential campaign. Roosevelt's candidacy split the Republican vote and helped Woodrow Wilson to be elected president.

 A Stiff Upper Lip: The Presidency

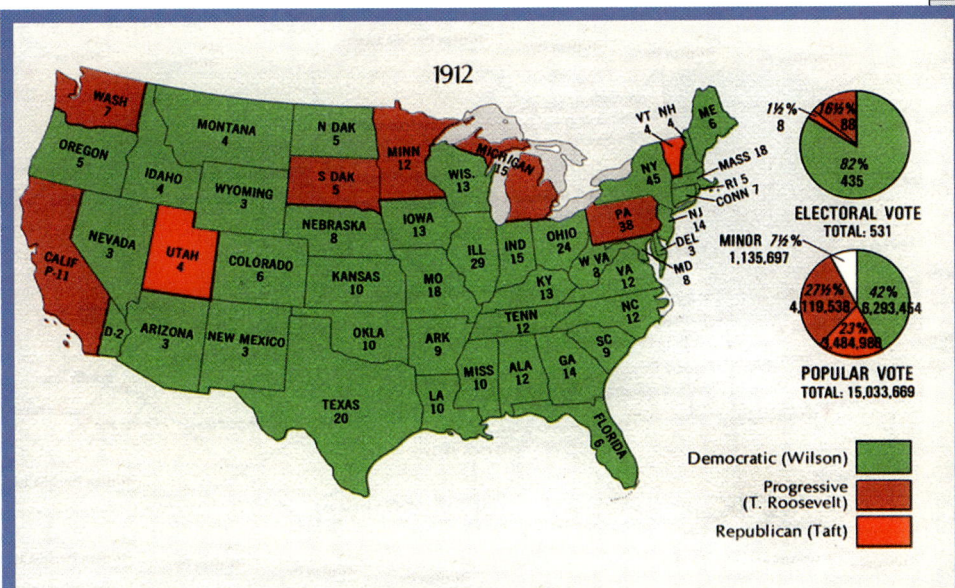

▲ This map shows Taft's overwhelming defeat in the 1912 election. Taft received only 8 electoral votes to Wilson's 435. Roosevelt came in second, with 88 electoral votes.

William Howard Taft, however, took his loss in stride. "I have held the office of President once, and that is more than most men have," he wrote to Nellie, "so I am content to retire from it with a consciousness that I have done the best I could."[4]

Chapter 5

From Yale to the Supreme Court, 1913–1930

In March 1913, for the first time in his adult life, William Howard Taft was out of work. It was not long before Taft's beloved Yale came through, however, offering Taft a position as a professor of law. When Taft and Nellie arrived on campus, they walked to Memorial Hall, where the famous professor gave a speech before the roaring crowd. "As I hear your cheers and songs I feel young again, as if I had shed some of my years," he said. "I come here wanting to help what little I can the young men who are going out into the nation."[1]

Taft was well-liked by his students, who would often see the former president borrowing books from the law library to prepare his lectures. But Taft was also hard on his students. He wrote an article in May 1914 for the *Ladies Home Journal* titled "The College Slouch." In it, he said that the lack of discipline he saw in young people was caused by a changing society in which government, religious education, and economics were all easily questioned.

Taft was a busy man during this time. In addition to teaching at Yale, he spoke at many bar association events. He was also appointed by Woodrow Wilson during World War I to serve as co-chairman of the National War Labor Board, which settled labor disputes that threatened to affect products needed for the war.

▶ A Reconciliation

Fate was about to bring Taft face to face with his former friend Theodore Roosevelt. At the funeral of a Yale professor,

From Yale to the Supreme Court

Taft saw Roosevelt for the first time since the election. Taft invited Roosevelt to come to his home afterward for a visit, but Roosevelt refused. However, the two men began exchanging letters. By chance, in May 1918, Taft and Roosevelt were both staying at the same hotel in Chicago. Roosevelt had stopped at the hotel for some dinner, on his way to Iowa to campaign for greater American participation in the war. Taft was headed east from St. Louis, where he had been working on the War Labor Board. When Taft heard that Roosevelt was in the dining room, he immediately headed to Roosevelt's table with his hand extended. Roosevelt accepted it with a wide grin. "Wasn't it a gracious

Although he had failed in his reelection bid, Taft soon busied himself by teaching law at Yale, where he was well-liked by his students.

The Old Senate Chamber, where the Court sat from 1860-1935 (photographer not known, c. 1900).

▲ During William Howard Taft's tenure as chief justice, the Supreme Court met in the Old Senate Chamber in the Capitol (pictured above). Taft succeeded in getting Congress to provide funding for the present Supreme Court Building to be built, and he hired its original architect, Cass Gilbert. Unfortunately, neither man lived to see the Court's permanent home completed, in 1935.

thing for him to do," Roosevelt said later. "I never felt happier over anything in my life.... I've seen old Taft and we're in perfect harmony on everything."[2]

Taft and Roosevelt reunited politically as well, working together to campaign for a Republican Congress. But their reunion was not to last for long. Roosevelt, whose health had been failing, died on January 6, 1919. William Howard Taft attended the simple funeral of his old friend in Oyster Bay, Long Island.

Fulfilling the Dream

On June 30, 1921, Taft received the message that would put his reelection defeat, his long feud with Roosevelt, and the other disappointments of his life behind him forever. At last, President Warren G. Harding appointed Taft chief justice of the United States. His lifelong ambition—to serve on the Supreme Court—was finally realized.

But when he assumed his new position, Taft found that the high court had a backlog of hundreds of cases. Almost immediately, he began a schedule of busy and long workdays, which began at 6 A.M. and lasted until 10 P.M. His only breaks were for meals and a midday walk from his home to the Capitol, which then housed the Supreme Court.

Achievements as Chief Justice

Taft realized that the only way for the Court to move through the cases was to create more unity among the justices' decisions. One of his greatest achievements as chief justice was his ability to control the other justices, who were often at odds with one another. He urged justices to vote with the majority, even if they disagreed, to keep from wasting time writing dissenting opinions. Part of the problem was that the Court was forced to hear any case from a lower federal court that involved the United States Constitution. In 1925, Taft pushed for an act of Congress that gave the Supreme Court greater power over which cases it would take. Taft also helped to create the Conference of Senior Circuit Court Judges, with the chief justice at the helm, which helped to make court systems more efficient.

Taft's most famous work included several cases that upheld the right of labor unions to strike against their employers, but also made sure that employers' rights were protected as well. In a rare case in which he disagreed with the majority of the Court, Taft argued in favor of a minimum wage law. Taft also successfully pushed Congress to provide funding for the Supreme Court to have its own building in Washington, D.C.

Taft's days on the Supreme Court were the happiest days of his life. "The truth is," Taft wrote, "that in my present life I don't remember that I ever was president."[3] In September 1927, he celebrated his seventieth birthday, surrounded by more than a hundred friends and family members.

Chapter 6 ▶

Last Years and Legacy

Although William Howard Taft's years as chief justice were fulfilling, his grueling schedule began to take its toll on his health. Taft had been overweight his entire life, and he developed heart disease. He suffered from small heart attacks and intestinal trouble, and his memory began to fail as well. Throughout his years on the Supreme Court,

▲ This photograph of Taft on a golf course in Hot Springs, Virginia, shows him enjoying a rare moment of relaxation.

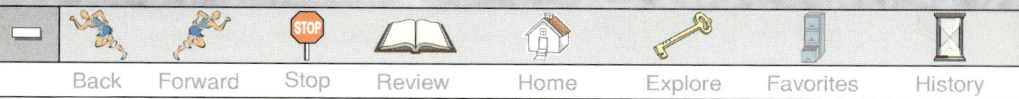

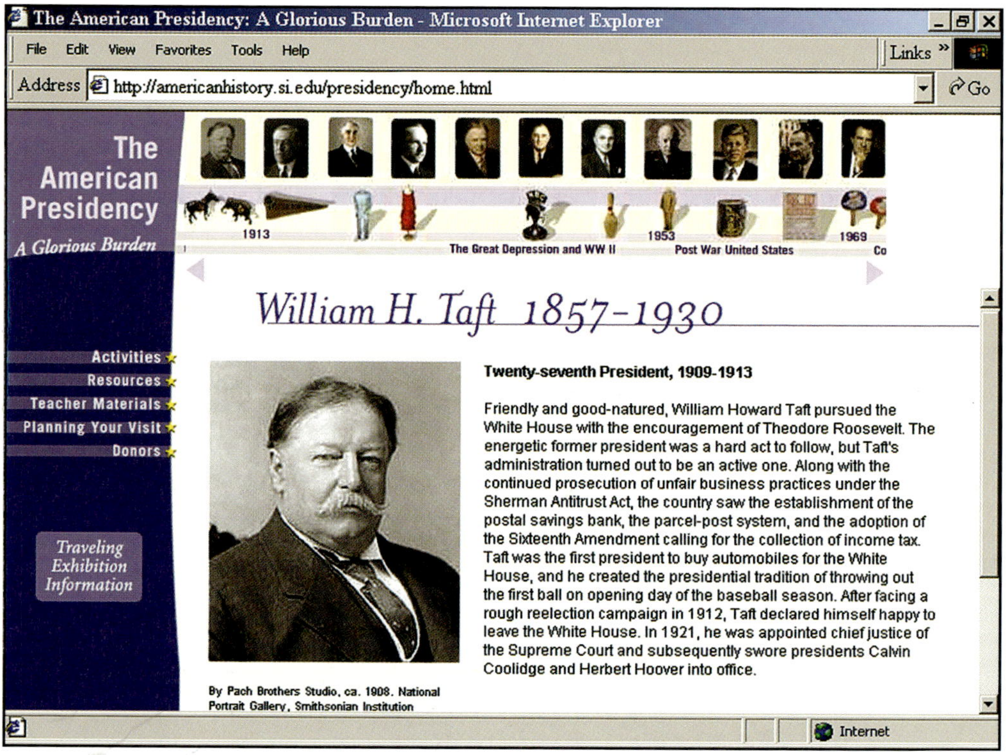
The American Presidency: A Glorious Burden - Microsoft Internet Explorer
File Edit View Favorites Tools Help
Links
Address http://americanhistory.si.edu/presidency/home.html
Go
The American Presidency
A Glorious Burden
1913
The Great Depression and WW II
1953
Post War United States
1969
Activities
Resources
Teacher Materials
Planning Your Visit
Donors
Traveling Exhibition Information
William H. Taft 1857–1930
Twenty-seventh President, 1909-1913
Friendly and good-natured, William Howard Taft pursued the White House with the encouragement of Theodore Roosevelt. The energetic former president was a hard act to follow, but Taft's administration turned out to be an active one. Along with the continued prosecution of unfair business practices under the Sherman Antitrust Act, the country saw the establishment of the postal savings bank, the parcel-post system, and the adoption of the Sixteenth Amendment calling for the collection of income tax. Taft was the first president to buy automobiles for the White House, and he created the presidential tradition of throwing out the first ball on opening day of the baseball season. After facing a rough reelection campaign in 1912, Taft declared himself happy to leave the White House. In 1921, he was appointed chief justice of the Supreme Court and subsequently swore presidents Calvin Coolidge and Herbert Hoover into office.
By Pach Brothers Studio, ca. 1908. National Portrait Gallery, Smithsonian Institution
Internet

The tradition of the president throwing out the ceremonial first pitch to usher in the Major League Baseball season began with Taft. He was asked by an umpire to perform that honor during the opening game of the 1910 season between the Washington Senators and Philadelphia Athletics. It is said that the seventh-inning stretch also originated with Taft that day, when he stood up to stretch his legs after the top of the seventh inning. Fans who saw him, and thought he was leaving, stood up also.

however, Taft carefully watched his diet, dropping to 244 pounds, about the same weight he had maintained as a college student at Yale. Nellie, who had been critical of Taft throughout their marriage, was more supportive during this time, often traveling to the local library to fetch Taft's favorite novels. But her attentions and his strict diet were not enough to save his failing health.

On New Year's Eve 1929, Taft's half brother Charles, whom he had always been close to, died in Cincinnati. Although Taft was not feeling well himself, he attended the funeral, further weakening his resistance. Upon his return to Washington, doctors ordered him to take a leave of absence from the Supreme Court to rest and recover. Taft only grew weaker. In February 1930, Taft regretfully submitted his resignation as chief justice to President Herbert Hoover. A month later, on March 8, 1930, William Howard Taft died at his home in Washington, D.C., at seventy-two years of age. He was buried in Arlington National Cemetery, in Virginia, the first president to be buried there. When Nellie Taft passed away, thirteen years later, she was buried by his side.

▶ A Tribute

One of the most moving tributes to Taft came in a letter signed by all the justices of the Supreme Court only weeks before his death. "You came to us from achievement in other fields and with the prestige of the illustrious place that you lately had held," the justices wrote, "and you showed us in new form your voluminous capacity for getting work done, your humor that smoothed the tough places, your golden heart that brought you love from every side and most of all from your brethren whose tasks you have made happy and light."[1]

▶ Taft's Legacy

William Howard Taft's life was spent in the pursuit of high office—mostly to gain the approval of his family and his peers. But sometimes this approval was hard to attain precisely because of Taft's fairness. He would not always side with the Republican Party, for example, if doing so meant

going against what he felt was the right decision. He is still respected for unifying and streamlining the Supreme Court. Taft's intelligence, dedication, and ambition were also reflected in the careers of his children. His son Robert went on to become a U.S. senator and a respected member of the Republican Party. His daughter, Helen, earned a Ph.D. in history and became an author and professor. And his youngest son, Charles, became mayor of Cincinnati.

To this day, William Howard Taft, the twenty-seventh president and former chief justice of the United States, remains the only person in American history to have achieved the highest offices of both the executive and judicial branches of government.

Chapter Notes

Chapter 1. The Reluctant President

1. Ishbel Ross, *An American Family: The Tafts—1678 to 1964* (Cleveland and New York: The World Publishing Company, 1964), p. 194.

2. Ibid.

3. PBS, *The American President*, "William Howard Taft," n.d., <http://www.americanpresident.org/KoTrain/Courses/WHT/WHT_Campaigns_and_Elections.htm> (June 24, 2002).

4. Alpheus Thomas Mason, *William Howard Taft: Chief Justice* (New York: Simon & Schuster, 1964), p. 33.

Chapter 2. Learning the Law: Taft's Early Life, 1857–1880

1. Ishbel Ross, *An American Family: The Tafts—1678 to 1964* (Cleveland and New York: The World Publishing Company, 1964), p. 27.

2. Henry F. Pringle, *The Life and Times of William Howard Taft*, vol. 1 (Hamden, Conn.: Archon Books, 1964), p. 22.

3. Ross, p. 67.

Chapter 3. The Way to the White House, 1880–1908

1. Henry F. Pringle, *The Life and Times of William Howard Taft*, vol. 1 (Hamden, Conn.: Archon Books, 1964), p. 62.

2. Ishbel Ross, *An American Family: The Tafts—1678 to 1964* (Cleveland and New York: The World Publishing Company, 1964), p. 88.

3. Pringle, p. 82.

4. Alpheus Thomas Mason, *William Howard Taft: Chief Justice* (New York: Simon & Schuster, 1964), p. 17.

Chapter 4. A Stiff Upper Lip: The Presidency, 1909–1913

1. Henry F. Pringle, *The Life and Times of William Howard Taft*, vol. 1 (Hamden, Conn.: Archon Books, 1964), p. 395.

2. Judith Icke Anderson, *William Howard Taft: An Intimate History* (New York: Norton, 1981), p. 23.

3. Paolo E. Coletta, *The Presidency of William Howard Taft* (Lawrence: The University Press of Kansas, 1973), p. 73.

4. Ibid., p. 262.

Chapter 5. From Yale to the Supreme Court, 1913–1930

1. Ishbel Ross, *An American Family: The Tafts—1678 to 1964* (Cleveland and New York: The World Publishing Company, 1964), p. 268.

2. Herbert S. Duffy, *William Howard Taft* (New York: Minton, Blach & Company, 1930), p. 309.

3. Henry F. Pringle, *The Life and Times of William Howard Taft*, vol. 2 (Hamden, Conn.: Archon Books, 1964), p. 960.

Chapter 6. Last Years and Legacy

1. Henry F. Pringle, *The Life and Times of William Howard Taft*, vol. 2 (Hamden, Conn.: Archon Books, 1964), p. 1,079.

Further Reading

Anderson, Judith Icke. *William Howard Taft: An Intimate History.* New York: Norton, 1981.

Black, Gilbert J., ed. *William Howard Taft, 1857–1930: Chronology—Documents—Bibliographical Aids.* Dobbs Ferry, N.Y.: Oceana Publications, 1970.

Burton, David H., et al. *The Collected Works of William Howard Taft*, 2 vols. Athens: Ohio University Press, 2001.

Casey, Jane Clark. *Encyclopedia of Presidents: William Howard Taft.* Chicago: Children's Press, 1989.

Coletta, Paolo E. *The Presidency of William Howard Taft.* Lawrence: The University Press of Kansas, 1973.

Duffy, Herbert S. *William Howard Taft.* Fort Washington, Pa.: Eastern National, 1998.

Falkof, Lucille. *William H. Taft: Twenty-seventh President of the United States.* Ada, Okla.: Garrett Educational Corporation, 1990.

Feinstein, Stephen. *The 1910s: From World War I to Ragtime Music.* Berkeley Heights, N.J.: Enslow Publishers, Inc., 2001.

Gay, Kathlyn. *Who's Running the Nation? How Corporate Power Threatens Democracy.* Danbury, Conn.: Franklin Watts, 1998.

Manners, William. *TR and Will: A Friendship that Split the Republican Party.* New York: Harcourt, Brace & World, 1969.

Mason, Alpheus Thomas. *William Howard Taft: Chief Justice.* New York: Simon & Schuster, 1964.

Ross, Ishbel. *An American Family: The Tafts—1678 to 1964.* Cleveland and New York: The World Publishing Company, 1964.

Index

A
Arlington National Cemetery, 43
Arthur, Chester A., 21

B
Ballinger, Richard, 31

C
Cincinnati, Ohio, 14, 15, 22, 23, 44

D
Democratic Party, 26, 34, 35

G
Grant, Ulysses S., 18

H
Harding, Warren G., 39
Harrison, Benjamin, 23
Hoover, Herbert, 43

I
Interstate Commerce Commission, 33

M
Mann-Elkins Act, 33
McKinley, William, 25, 26

N
National War Labor Board, 36, 37

O
Ohio Superior Court, 23

P
Panama Canal, 27, 33
Payne-Aldrich Tariff Act, 31
Phillipines, 25–26, 28, 29
Pinchot, Gifford, 31
Progressive (Bull Moose) Party, 34

R
Republican Party, 20, 24, 25, 34, 43, 44
Roosevelt, Theodore, 11–12, 25, 26, 27, 28–29, 31, 33–34, 36–38

S
Sixth U.S. Circuit Court of Appeals, 25
Spanish-American War, 25
Supreme Court, United States, 11, 13, 23, 25, 33, 39–40, 41, 43–44

T
Taft, Alfonso (father), 14–15, 16, 21
Taft, Charles (son), 11, 25, 44
Taft, Helen (daughter), 25, 44
Taft, Helen Herron "Nellie" (wife), 11–12, 21–22, 23, 27, 30, 31–32, 35, 36, 42–43
Taft, Louise (mother), 14–15
Taft, Robert (son), 25, 44

U
U.S. Department of the Interior, 31
U.S. Forest Service, 31
U.S. Steel, 31

W
Wilson, Woodrow, 34, 36

Y
Yale University, 17, 18, 19, 36